ISBN 0 86163 189 7

Copyright ©1987 Award Publications Limited

First Published 1987

Published by Award Publications Limited,
Spring House, Spring Place,
London, NW5 3BH

Printed in Belgium

MORE BIBLE STORIES

RETOLD BY JANE CARRUTH

*Illustrated
by
Rene Cloke*

AWARD PUBLICATIONS
LONDON

Long ago, in Nazareth, a young Jewish girl called Mary was visited by an angel from God. The angel told her that she would have a baby who would be the Saviour of the world. 'His name shall be Jesus,' the angel said.

The wonderful baby was soon to be born when Mary and her husband, Joseph the carpenter, made the long journey to Bethlehem to pay their taxes to the Roman Governor who ruled their country. Joseph could find nowhere for Mary to rest until one of the innkeepers offered them shelter in the stable where he kept his animals.

That night Jesus was born, and Mary wrapped him in swaddling clothes and laid him in a manger.

That same night some shepherds were guarding their sheep in the fields outside Bethlehem when they saw a bright light in the dark sky. The shepherds were frightened at first but they soon lost their fear when an angel appeared and told them of the birth of Jesus, the King.

'We must find this King and worship him,' they told each other, as a heavenly choir of angels began praising God. And the shepherds ran down the slopes into the town where they found the baby in the stable.

Now, far away, three wise men learned from the stars in the heavens that a King had been born and, with a bright new star to guide them, they set out on their camels to find him.

When they reached Jerusalem, where cruel King Herod lived, they asked about the new King. As Herod listened he grew troubled and jealous. 'I know nothing about this infant king,' he said at last, hiding his fears. 'When you find him, come back and tell me!'

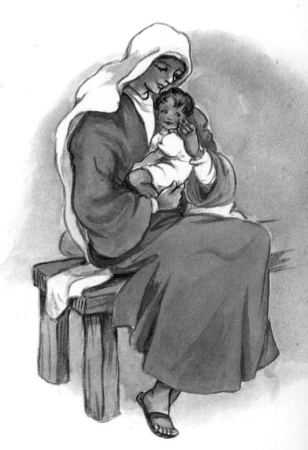

The bright new star guided the wise men to the stable in Bethlehem, where they found baby Jesus with his mother, Mary. They presented the baby with the rich treasures they had brought with them and bowed down before him. But, instead of returning to Jerusalem to report to Herod that they had found the King, they went back to their own country by another way.

King Herod waited anxiously for the wise men to come to him
with news of the child born to be King. When they did not
appear, he sent out his soldiers with orders to kill all baby boys
under two years old. But Joseph had already been warned in a
dream to take Mary and her baby to the land of Egypt where
they would be in no danger from Herod's soldiers.

They stayed in Egypt until Joseph was told, in another dream,
that Herod was dead and it was safe to return home. And so they
went back to Nazareth, that little town in Galilee where Jesus
lived nearly all his life.

One day, when he was twelve years old, Mary and Joseph took Jesus to Jerusalem for the greatest festival of the year, the Feast of the Passover. When it was time to leave, Jesus was missing. It was only after three days of anxious searching that they found him in the temple talking to the wise teachers. 'You should not have worried,' Jesus told his mother. 'You should have known I would be here in the temple, which is my Father's house!'

Jesus did not begin telling the people about God, his Father in heaven, until he was about thirty years old. But, a man called John the Baptist, preached that the Son of God would soon be among them. Those who believed John were baptised in the River Jordan. One day Jesus himself asked to be baptised. John agreed and as Jesus left the water the heavens opened and a beautiful dove came down and rested on Jesus. This was a sign to John that Jesus was truly the Son of God.

Jesus had many friends among the fishermen who lived close to the Sea of Galilee. Once, as he walked along the shore he came to a boat manned by two brothers, Simon Peter and Andrew.

'Will you leave your boat and follow me?' Jesus asked. And the brothers did so at once.

A little further on Jesus came upon two more brothers, James and John. They were busy mending their nets with the help of their old father Zebedee. 'Leave your nets and come with me,' Jesus called out.

The brothers did not hesitate. They said goodbye to their father and went with Jesus.

These four fishermen were the first disciples. They stayed with Jesus and never left him.

Jesus loved his mother and to please her he performed his first miracle. Friends had invited them to a wedding feast in Cana, some miles from home. When all the guests were enjoying themselves, Mary whispered to Jesus, 'Our friends are upset. There is no more wine.'

Jesus went to the servants. 'Fill the six stone jars with water,' he told them. 'And then fill the empty wine-pitchers.'

The servants obeyed. Imagine their surprise when out of the pitchers came very good wine instead of water!

One day an important man called Jairus came to Jesus and begged him to save his daughter, who was dying. On the way to his house, word came that the child was already dead. The house was filled with the sound of weeping but Jesus comforted the father, saying, 'She is not dead, but sleeping.' Then he stood over the child and took her hand.

'Rise up!' he said. And, to the wonder and joy of her parents, the little girl got up.

Jesus spent his days teaching the people about God, his Father, and working miracles. He gave the blind back their sight, and made the lame and sick strong again. Wherever he went crowds followed him, and many believed that they had only to touch the hem of his robe to be made well again. And, because they had faith, Jesus healed them.

One morning Jesus was so tired that his disciples persuaded him to go to a quiet, deserted place to rest. But a huge crowd, men, women and children, followed him. Jesus talked to them most of the day, until night fell. The disciples wanted Jesus to send the people away.

'Let them go back to their villages,' they said. 'We cannot hope to feed such a crowd.' But Jesus did not want to see them go away hungry. Then Andrew, one of the disciples, said, 'Master, there is a boy here who has five loaves and two fishes.'

Jesus said, 'Make the people sit down on the grass.' Then he took the loaves and fishes and blessed them, and broke them up, and the disciples had enough food to satisfy the huge, hungry crowd of five thousand people. And afterwards there were enough pieces of bread left over for the disciples to fill twelve baskets!

Sometimes Jesus told stories to help his listeners understand the lesson he was teaching. One day he told them a story about a traveller who was attacked by fierce robbers and left for dead by the roadside.

Two other travellers on that lonely road came along, a priest and a Levite, but neither of them stopped to help the wounded man. Then came a Samaritan. The Samaritan bound up the stranger's wounds and took him to the nearest inn on the back of his mule. 'Here is money to pay for his keep,' the Samaritan told the innkeeper. 'Take care of him.'

'Now which of these three men was a neighbour to the wounded traveller?' Jesus asked his listeners.

'Why, the good Samaritan!' came back the answer.

'Then be a good neighbour like him!' Jesus said.

Another story Jesus told was all about forgiveness. A rich man had two sons. The younger asked for his share of his father's wealth and left home to have a good time. He ended up so poor and hungry that he took a job of looking after pigs. 'I will go home and ask my father to forgive me,' he decided at last.

The father was so happy to see his long-lost son that he forgave him at once and treated him like an honoured guest. The elder brother was so jealous that he stayed away from the celebrations.

'God is like the father in the story,' Jesus said. 'He forgives all sinners who are sorry and return to him.'

Once Jesus told a story about the people of his Father's Kingdom.

A sower went out to sow his seeds. Some seed fell on the path and was soon eaten by birds. Some fell on rocky ground and sprouted but quickly withered and died because it had no proper roots. Some fell among thorn bushes which choked the seedlings. But there was some seed which fell on good ground. And in time this grain grew into a wonderful golden harvest.

'Those people who listen to God and understand his message,' Jesus said at the end of his story, 'are like the good ground. They will enter into the Kingdom of Heaven.'

Jesus loved little children. They would greet him as a friend and he would bless them with gentle kindness. 'The Kingdom of Heaven is made up of such as these,' he told his disciples when they would have sent them away.

Sometimes, when he was tired, Jesus visited the house of Martha and Mary, two sisters who lived with their young brother, Lazarus. Jesus was a long way from their village when the sad news reached him that Lazarus had died. He set out to be with them and Martha ran to greet him when he arrived and took him to the tomb. Lazarus had been dead four days but Jesus, out of pity, brought him back to life and restored him to the sisters.

Towards the end of his short life on earth, Jesus entered Jerusalem riding on a young donkey. The people were so happy to see him that they spread branches of palm trees in the donkey's path. Soon a great procession had formed and the crowd sang, 'Blessed is the King who has come in the name of the Lord!'

When he was in Jerusalem Jesus went to the splendid golden temple which had been built to give glory to God, his Father. How angry he was when he found the traders had turned the temple court into a market-place, selling pigeons and changing money.

'You have made my Father's house of prayer into a den of thieves!' he cried. And overturning some of the tables, he drove the traders away.

In Jerusalem there were men who hated Jesus because he claimed to be the Son of God. The chief priests and the scribes had been trying to find a way to capture Jesus secretly when Judas Iscariot came to them. Judas, who was a disciple of Jesus, offered to betray his Master. 'How much will you give me,' he asked, 'if I deliver him into your hands?'

'Thirty pieces of silver,' came the answer. And well satisfied with his bargain, Judas accepted the money.

The next day, Jesus and his twelve disciples had supper in Jerusalem in a quiet room specially prepared for them. Jesus blessed the bread and wine they were to share together and then told his friends that he was soon to die. He already knew that Judas, who was present at the supper, had betrayed him to his enemies.

After the supper Jesus and the disciples went to a small garden of olive trees, where it was very peaceful. Jesus prayed a long time to his Father in heaven. Then came the soldiers, destroying the peace of the little garden. And, at a sign from Judas, they arrested Jesus and took him away.

Jesus was taken before Pontius Pilate, the Roman governor. Pilate could not find him guilty of any crime but that made no difference. Jesus was cruelly beaten by the Roman soldiers, and crowned with thorns, before being led away to be crucified in the company of two thieves.

Mary, his mother, and some of his friends kept watch by the cross. But there were others who made fun of him.

Jesus prayed aloud for his enemies as he hung on the cross.

'Father, forgive them, for they know not what they do,' he prayed.

When Jesus was taken down from the cross his body was laid in a new tomb cut out of solid rock, and a great stone was rolled across the entrance.

Among the women who visited the tomb was Mary Magdalene. How sad and frightened she was when she found the heavy stone rolled away and the tomb empty. As she stood there weeping, a young man she mistook for the gardener, spoke to her in a voice she knew at once. 'Mary!' he said.

'Master!' Mary cried. And she knelt down at the feet of Jesus.

Jesus had told his closest friends many times that he would rise from the dead. And now his presence among them filled them with joy.

One day he appeared on the lakeside and stood watching Peter and his companions hard at work, fishing. They did not recognise Jesus when they returned with empty nets. And when he told them to try again they did so with bad grace.

What a catch they had! They thought their nets would break with all the fish. And it was only then that they knew the stranger on the shore was Jesus himself.

That day Jesus shared a simple meal of fish and bread with them and, listening to his words, they were like new men again, especially Peter.

'You must take care of my flock,' Jesus told him.

Jesus did not live with his friends as he had done before, but he appeared many times to them and a great number of his followers saw him and heard him speak.

At the end of forty days, he told his disciples that he must leave them and go to his Father in heaven. For the last time he talked to them about the Kingdom of God and the love his Father had for them. Then he led them out of Jerusalem towards a little town called Bethany and from there up the slopes of the Mount of Olives.

As they knelt on the hillside Jesus blessed them and, even while he did so, he was lifted up and a cloud received him out of their sight.

The disciples were not sad after Jesus left them. They knew he was the Son of God and he would be with them always.

Hope and courage filled their hearts as they began preparing for the great work Jesus had left them to do. 'Go and teach all nations,' Jesus had told them. And that is what they set out to do.